RAISING A CHILD is the most awesome responsibility any one of us can ever take on; nonetheless, it
doesn't have to be difficult. The secret, says nati
known family psychologist and parenting author
Rosemond, is getting in touch with your commor
John's down-to-earth advice has helped thousand
ents do exactly that. You'll find these nuggets of I
enting wisdom to be not only inspirational and th
provoking, but humorous as well—just what you
"stay the course" through the inevitable ups and
of parenthood. Enjoy!

Once upon a time, people got married, had children, and reared 'em. It wasn't something they spent a lot of time fussing and fretting over. And despite their relatively relaxed approach, they managed to do a good job.

If what I've said herein sounds old-fashioned, that's because it is. It's time we realized that thirty-plus years of "nouveau parenting" hasn't worked. It's high time we brought "old-fashioned" back into fashion in the family. Amen.

By taking good care of their marriages, married parents are taking good care of their children. By taking good care of themselves, single parents are taking good care of their children.

As a parent, you'll never be perfect, but you'll always be the only mother or father your child will ever want. Take that as a vote of confidence and do your best, because your best is always and forever going to be good enough.

Having multiple caretakers — each with a different personality and, therefore, different expectations — isn't confusing to a child. Confusing is when any one of those caretakers has one expectation one minute, another the next.

Being rewarded for **not** misbehaving teaches a child that adults will offer you special things only if you misbehave. In other words, rewards often teach children that misbehavior pays.

Any teacher worth her salt establishes three understandings with her students: First, they will give her their undivided attention; second, they will do as she says; third, because she says so. Parents would do well to follow this example.

Prefixes and qualifiers like "step-" and "adopted" only get in the way. They are un-necessary distractions. Parents are parents, and children are children, period.

Once upon a time, parents put their marriages first, expected children to obey, assigned them chores, and said "no" more than "yes." Some call this old-fashioned. I call it tried-and-true.

Did my wife and I, when our children were young, "dictate" to them? The dictionary says that means "to instruct with authority." We are, therefore, guilty as charged.

On the one hand, parents worry about peer pressure during the teen years. On the other, they don't want their children to do without anything their children's friends have. An example of one hand not knowing what the other is doing.

It took me years to realize that grandparents do no harm by "spoiling." In fact, I'm now convinced that it's as proper for grandparents to spoil grandchildren as it is **improper** for parents to do likewise.

If you think childrearing is difficult,
it will be.

Staying married: There is no struggle in life so tough, and nothing else in life so worth the struggle.

Contrary to the myth, previous generations of women were not home **with** their children. They were home **for** their children. They supervised, but did not pay lots of attention or become highly involved. And their kids did just fine.

Every child is gifted. Every child is talented. Unfortunately, programs for "gifted and talented children" fail to recognize those facts.

Stripping away all the intellectual rhetoric and the flowery sentiment, the purpose of raising children is to help them out of our lives and into successful lives of their own. It's called emancipation.

Seemingly harmless programs like "Sesame Street" have led today's children to equate entertainment and education. They come to school expecting to be entertained, and when they're not, they complain that school is "boring."

In the last forty years or so, we've done such a good job of turning wives into mothers and husbands into bread-winners/dads that by the time their children leave home, they've often forgotten how to be married.

This business about letting children "express their feelings" disturbs me. Feelings are private matters, not meant for public display. Teaching a child to control the expression of a feeling is not the same as teaching that the feeling is bad.

The language of television-watching conceals its reality. People talk about watching television "together," but the two things — watching television and togetherness — are mutually exclusive. You always watch television alone.

Today's parents, most of whom seem to believe childrearing is **hard,** have been encouraged to think too much about it. All this thinking drowns out the voice of common-sense. They think, think, think; therefore, it's hard.

Television is the single greatest threat to communication and intimacy within a family. You may as well be fifty miles away from the person sitting next to you if you're both watching television.

Ricky Nelson never talked back to Ozzie and Harriet. Today, it's "funny" if a child-star on a TV sit-com talks back to his parents. This does nothing but reinforce the dangerous notion that disrespect for adults is not just normal, but harmless.

Men are just as important as women to the raising of children. Unfortunately, childrearing is still thought of as primarily "woman's work." As a result, there is a general tendency to regard fathers as mere "parenting aides."

Parents once spoke in "parenting shorthand." They said things like "children should be seen and not heard," "you can't have your cake and eat it too," "you make your bed, you lie in it." How absolutely non-intellectual. How absolutely refreshing!

In the eyes of a child, parents are "mean" when the child discovers that they **mean** what they say.

The publicity surrounding the so-called "strong-willed" child has been almost exclusively negative. The impression is that they come from the bottom of the behavioral barrel. Well, I ask, who would want a weak-willed kid? Not me!

If you want a child to make unreasonable demands, act "starved" for attention, take you for granted, be disrespectful and disobedient, simply give him a lot and expect little in return.

Parental authority must be clearly established before the full potential for affection within the parent-child relationship can be released. Unresolved disciplinary issues create stress in a family. Resolve them, and relationships will be more relaxed.

If, instead of enforcing rules dispassionately, a basketball referee threatened, gave second chances, and made deals, the game would become a free-for-all. The same will happen in a family when parents threaten, give second chances, and make deals.

DAILY GUIDE TO PARENTING   JAN. 16

Love is not necessarily warm and fuzzy. To love a child is to act in the child's best interest. Discipline, therefore, is love. Expecting a child to do chores around the home is love. Not giving a child a lot of material things is love.

Permissive and authoritarian parents are more alike than dissimilar. Neither, for example can think straight when it comes to children. The former's ability to do so is obstructed by worry and guilt; the latter's by anger.

My mother expected me to play outside, weather permitting, and she defined "weather permitting" very liberally. I played with other children who'd been kicked out of their houses. Being out from "underfoot" was great for both mothers and their kids!

Children need a lot of supervision, but not a lot of attention. Too much attention, like too much of any other initially good thing, is addictive.

Too many parents fool around with misbehavior. They're too concerned with the punishment fitting the "crime," not realizing that a punishment doesn't fit a crime unless it stops the crime from happening.

When parents treat a child as if he or she was their equal, they will be unable to convince the child of their authority. A child cannot look **up** and straight ahead at the same time.

A spanking properly administered by a parent is an act of authority, but a spanking administered by a teacher is an act of desperation, and children know the difference.

Limit your child's inclusion in adult activities, and limit your involvement in your child's activities. It's easier for a child to look up to parents who have lives of their own.

Previous generations of parents believed children should fight their own battles, do their own homework, figure out how to occupy themselves. This enabled children to take responsibility for themselves and learn to stand on their own two feet.

You don't have to hide all of your conflicts from your children. Children need to learn that conflict and intimacy are inseparable; that conflict can be creative rather than destructive. If you don't teach them these things, who will?

The best part of the "empty nest syndrome" is when the children call home to tell you they miss you and want to spend time with you during semester break. The second-best part is when break is over and they leave again.

Children who learn to separate comfortably from their parents at bedtime are better prepared to separate from them under other circumstances as well.

The "empty nest syndrome" means always being able to find a parking space in the driveway, not waiting up until the children get home, picking up the phone and the line is free, the refrigerator has food in it .... This is cause for depression?

The more **interesting** a person you are, the more attention your children will pay to you. Children are fascinated by adults who have lots of interests. They are **not** fascinated by adults who pay a lot of attention to them.

Teaching children about "safe sex" is as absurd as teaching them how to use drugs without getting addicted or how to drink without getting drunk.

It is impossible to parent well from a position of self-sacrifice; good parenting can only be accomplished from a position of self-fulfillment.

Children cannot understand an adult point-of-view. Furthermore, they aren't really interested. If they were, they'd **listen** instead of interrupting when we tried to explain ourselves.

DAILY GUIDE TO PARENTING   DEC.8

If you expect children to obey, they will. If you threaten them if they don't obey, they'll obey — until your back is turned, that is.

Where toys are concerned, less is more — more imagination, more creativity, more initiative, more resourcefulness, more improvisation. In short, more fun!

You can win an argument only with someone who can understand and therefore be swayed by your point-of-view. That's why parents cannot win arguments with children. A child will understand a parent's point-of-view when he's a parent. No sooner.

The feeling of being bored, of having nothing to do, has nothing to do with being a child. Rather, it has to do with being a child of the present generation. Where children are not over-indulged, they are not bored.

Most of the decisions parents make are arbitrary. They are matters of personal preference, not universal absolutes. That's why "because I said so" is usually the most honest answer a parent can give a child asking "why?" or "why not?"

Once upon a time, children did what they were told because they were told. This was before the "experts" informed us that "because I said so" had destroyed the self-esteem of entire generations.

A **benevolent dictatorship** is a form of family government in which parents recognize that their foremost responsibility is that of providing equal measures of love (benevolence) and authority (dictation) to their children.

Many children are of the impression — honestly gained — that they do not have to do as they are told unless (1) adults give them "good" reasons, and (2) they will be amply rewarded for cooperating.

Benevolently dictatorial parents don't derive sadistic pleasure out of bossing children around. They simply recognize that it's every child's right to be governed well, and every parent's responsibility to provide good government.

Did you watch "Sesame Street" as a child? Probably not. Yet you learned to read! Amazing! Children do not need to watch so-called "educational" programs in order to become educated!

In a benevolent dictatorship, as children mature, they are honored with increasing responsibility and privilege. In a **malevolent** dictatorship, children have no honor.

When a child says he doesn't have an explanation for some misbehavior, he's probably telling the truth. By continuing to press for an explanation, you just might get a lie.

Within the ever-expanding framework of limits created for them by benevolently dictatorial parents, children learn that freedom and responsibility go hand-in-hand.

If your child accuses you of being "mean,"
you must have done something right.

Parents cannot effectively communicate their love to a child unless they are also a source of effective authority.

In the final analysis, the ability to laugh — at oneself, at the things children do — is the very best of all parenting qualities.

Parents cannot effectively discipline unless they are also a source of genuine love. Put another way, a child will not seek to please someone who cannot be pleased.

Teachers who encourage parents to help children with their homework are unwittingly shooting themselves in the foot. A child who knows his parents are going to help with homework is a child who doesn't have to pay attention in class.

Authority provides direction and self-discipline to a child. Love provides meaning and a sense of belonging. Together, they provide the child with a stable, secure sense of who he is and is capable of becoming.

In the parent-child relationship, empowerment is a two-way street. To fully empower a child to take eventual control of his life, parents must properly assume the awesome power of parenthood.

Have you ever noticed? Truly obedient children — children who have invested great amounts of security and, therefore, respect in their parents' authority — are also the world's happiest, most outgoing, and creative kids.

Self-sufficiency is the yardstick of self-esteem. The road to self-sufficiency is paved with frustration, disappointment, failure, falling flat on one's face, and other equally "unhappy" experiences. We cannot afford to deny children these things.

Children show respect for parents by obeying them. Parents show respect for children by expecting them to obey.

If you are so determined, you can indeed keep a child happy for eighteen years. In the process, you will surely destroy the child's self-esteem. Why? Because self-esteem is reflected in the child's belief that "I can do it myself!"

A young child needs to believe that there are virtually no limits to his parents' capabilities. This "immature" belief in their omnipotence anchors the child's sense of security, enabling the growth of competence.

Hobbies, now all-but completely replaced by adult-organized after-school activities, are expressions of individuality, accomplishment, perseverance, and goal-setting. These survival skills are every child's birthright.

A child who constantly tests limits is doing nothing more than trying to pin down parents who don't know where they should stand.

When parents give to a child all that he needs and a small amount of what he simply wants, the child is forced to figure things out for himself. Therein lie the roots of perseverance and resourcefulness.

Consistency makes it possible for a child to predict the consequences of his or her behavior. The child who can't predict what his parents are going to do from one misbehavior to the next cannot learn to control his misbehavior.

On average, children want ten times more attention, toys, freedom, and so on than they actually need. About the only things today's child needs more of than he or she wants are chores and consequences.

Discipline is more than just an occasional act. It's a theme that should run through every aspect of the parent-child relationship.

To a child, **need** and **want** feel exactly the same. The child will remain forever confused unless parents do a good job of separating the wheat from the chaff, the necessary from the unnecessary.

To be an effective disciplinarian, you must be a model of self-discipline.

Parents don't rear children anymore. They **parent**. The noun and the verb, the person and the process, have become one and the same. The implication: raising a child is all-consuming, laborious; to do it well, you must devote yourself to it.

A matter-of-fact attitude toward discipline creates a calm, relaxed atmosphere in which everyone's "place" is clear. This allows life within a family to be simple, as it should be.

The chorus of complaint about how difficult it is to raise children is unique to this generation of parents. Implicit to this griping is the strange notion that if childrearing isn't wearing you out, you must not be working at it hard enough.

Self-confidence, not technique, is the key to successful discipline. Without self-confidence, no technique will work. With self-confidence, little technique is necessary.

The more responsibility a parent assumes for homework, the less the child will assume. The more help the parent provides, the more helpless the child will act. Under the circumstances, failure is inevitable. The only question is "when?"

Good parents take very, very good care
of their marriage, lest their marriage
become a mirage.

If, because your parents said it a lot when you were a child, you can't bring yourself to say "because I said so," try "because decisions of this sort can only be made by grown-ups" or "because I am the parent, you are the child."
Same difference.

In a family in which there are two adults — one male, one female — the relationship that requires the greatest amount of "quality time" is the marriage.

Many so-called "insecure" children are lacking, not in love or adequate attention, but discipline. Many of them, in fact, have been getting far too much attention for far too long.

Expecting children to obey involves having a plan for what you're going to do if they don't. In fact, the secret to virtually frustration-free discipline is, first, have a plan; then, carry it through consistently.

A woman, while taking care of her children, is fulfilling her responsibilities. Her husband, when he takes care of the children, is "babysitting." What!? They're not his kids!?

The most effective time for dealing with misbehavior is **before** it occurs. By anticipating the misdeed and deciding, in advance, how you're going to respond, you keep your balance (and your cool) when it occurs.

Many women, regardless of marital status, possess a "single-parent mentality," meaning they mistakenly believe the outcome of the childrearing process rests on their shoulders, and their shoulders alone.

The more a child sees that his or her misbehavior "upsets" a parent, the more the child will misbehave, but not by choice. The parent's loss of balance creates an unresolved issue, which the child is driven to resolve by doing more of the same.

A learning-disabled child may have to put more time and effort into mastering certain tasks, but is still capable of mastery. Excusing the child from frustrating tasks is a sure way of turning disability into inability.

Many parents think that for any given disciplinary situation, there is but one correct course of action. The fact is, the **manner** in which parents convey a disciplinary action is far more important than the action itself.

Today's parent seems compelled to provide explanations when children demand to know "why!?" or "why not!?" Despite the obvious fact that explanations serve no purpose other than a child's need to argue, parents continue to provide them.

Trust your feelings and intuitions. Stop worrying that you're going to traumatize your child for life if you make a bad decision. Bad decisions don't do long-term damage; bad **people** do.

A child won't have the wherewithall to "just say no" to drugs, alcohol, and sex if his or her parents aren't capable of saying no to new video-game cartridges, the latest in stereo hardware, new cars, the latest designer clothes, and so on.

The manner in which a child is disciplined will shape his or her attitudes toward men and women. For this reason, discipline should be handled such that children do not view their fathers as "heavies" and their mothers as "pushovers" (or vice versa).

A good general chooses his battles carefully, knows that retreat can be strategic, and knows you must sometimes lose a battle in order to win the war. Parents would do wise to apply these same ideas to the raising of children.

Beware of truisms. Often enough, truisms turn out to be false-isms, and this is particularly the case concerning the pseudo-science of "parenting."

A woman with children who works outside of her home is called a working **mother**. A man with children who works outside his home is called a carpenter or a mechanic or a doctor. He has a career; she has a problem.

Like sugar, praise can be habit-forming. Children who are praised excessively eventually begin to act like they "can't get enough." Ironically, the over-effort to make them "feel good about themselves" eventually causes them to act insecure.

Some parents pin their sense of adequacy to their children's behavior. When their children misbehave, they ask "What did we do wrong?" As a result, their children don't have to accept responsibility for their own misbehavior.

Praise is not something to be tossed out carelessly. Be conservative and thoughtful about it. Above all else, with praise as with punishment, take aim at the act, not the child.

Many parents, when confronted with misbehavior, think in terms of "what should I do?" instead of "what should I say?" They don't realize that good communication is more important to effective discipline than punishment.

Indecisive parents are afraid of making mistakes. They think bad decisions scar children for life, so they end up making no decisions at all; and **that's** the biggest mistake a parent can ever make.

Following divorce, many single parents center their lives around their children, forming what amounts to a primary relationship with them. This virtually guarantees that those children will become ever-more demanding and uncooperative.

Abiding love and consistent authority are the cornerstones of a child's sense of well-being. One without the other makes for a weak foundation.

A child who, upon testing a rule, is able to verify its actual existence, is then free to operate creatively and constructively within its boundaries. Rules, therefore, help children become more intelligent.

A pop to a child's rear end is useful only as a form of nonverbal communication. It's an exclamation point of sorts, placed in **front** of an important message. It is **not** a message in and of itself.

A rule is not a rule unless it is enforced consistently. Otherwise, it is a wish, a fraud, and a child so misgoverned is a prisoner of uncertainty.

A pop to a child's rear end can serve as a reminder of authority and demonstration of disapproval. But a pop is absolutely worthless unless the parent follows through with some other, more effective method of discipline.

If you act like you don't know where to stand and don't know where you want your child to stand, your child must test and test and test and keep on testing until the proverbial cows come home. We call this the "strong-willed child." Ha!

Grandparents can and should be one of a child's most valuable resources. At their best, grandparents are gentle teachers of the way life was and forever should be.

In past generations, children were not generally afraid of their parents. They respected them and, therefore, paid attention to them. Because children were paying attention, a stern **look** from a parent often said more than enough.

There are no quick fixes in childrearing. You can get a meal in a minute at McDonald's, but there's no such thing as McParenting.

Times have always changed, but we did not change our ideas about childrearing until after World War II. That's when we stopped listening to grandma and began listening to so-called "helping" professionals. And that's when our troubles began.

In the short span of one generation, we have managed to misplace a very important tenet of childrearing. Simply stated, it is that children, from an early age, should be responsible, contributing members of their families.

"No" is one of the most character-building words in the English language. Say it often, and mean it.

As parents, we have an obligation to endow our children with the skills they will need to lead successful adult lives. One of those skills is respect for others, which a child begins to develop by first learning to respect his or her parents.

Parents need to first draw a line between what children need and what they want; then they need to give them everything they truly need and a smattering of what they simply want. More than a smattering is over-indulgence.

Children need to learn that the reward of membership in a family is ultimately a matter of how they give of themselves to the family, not in what their parents give to them.

The Balance Beam of Parenting:
To be lovingly authoritative as well as authoritatively loving. To walk with this balance is to walk with grace.

The Agony Principle: Parents should never agonize over anything a child does or fails to do if the child is perfectly capable of agonizing over it himself.

It is important that the worlds of adults and children be distinct and often exclusive. Adults should interact primarily with other adults; children with other children.

The most effective parents are not those who are constantly busy in their children's lives, but those who are relaxed and create, therefore, a relaxed environment in which their children can be relaxed enough to discover their potential.

Raising a child — **parenting**, as it's now known — is not an intellectual exercise. In fact, the more you think and read about it, the more complicated it will seem and the less you will enjoy it.

Some of the most valuable lessons in life are learned courtesy of falling flat on one's face; or, as my father used to put it, "the hard way."

The only way a child can develop a tolerance for frustration is to experience it in realistic measure, thereby learning to accept it and overcome it.

Almost all learning is accomplished through trial-and-error. Therefore, lest parents prevent too much valuable learning, they should not prevent very much error.

Self-esteem is not something adults can bestow upon children. It is something children work toward and discover for themselves. We can support their work, but we cannot do it for them.

Parents who want their children to eventually stand on their own two feet must be occasionally willing to let them fall down.

Employers know that if they stand over employees, those employees will be resentful and less productive. Parents who feel they must stand over their children to get them to do chores or homework achieve the same results.

If, when your child forgets his books, you're willing to run after the bus, your child has no reason to ever remember his books.

"How many times have I told you not to do so-and-so?" means the parent failed to convince the child the first time. This is a parenting problem, not a child problem.

If, when your child does something "bad," **you** feel bad about it, your child won't.

It is said that the key to training a horse is to "make the right thing easy, the wrong thing hard." The same often applies to the rearing of children.

Ask a child no questions, the child will tell you no lies.

The Teenager's Creed:
It is less risky to ask for forgiveness than to ask for permission.

If you **think** your child did something, he probably did. If you're wrong, which you won't often be, apologize, but lose no faith in your intuitions.

There is no such thing as an argumentative child. There are only adults who enter into argument with children.

You can't teach a child how to act without also teaching the child what you want him to think. It's called passing on your values, which you cannot do by mincing either words or action.

Each of us is imperfect. Therefore, all marriages are imperfect, as are the families that result. This is not dysfunction; it's the struggle of life. We need fewer people who complain about it, and more who will commit themselves to it.

In order for children to become successful at the three "R's" of reading, 'riting, and 'rithmetic, parents must first teach them the **Three R's** of Respect, Responsibility, and Resourcefulness. These, not high IQ, define the **educable** child.

Anything you stand over a child to do, the child will not do. Tell a child what you expect, then walk away, leaving the "ball" in the child's court.

A child who has learned to pay attention to his or her parents will come to school prepared to pay attention to teachers.

God did not intend for married couples to be parents first, husband and wife second. That's why the marriage vow reads "...'til death do us part" and not "...'til children do us part."

Frustration, said many childrearing "experts," is bad for children. As a result of their parents' efforts to protect them from it, children became increasingly demanding, while their parents became increasingly frustrated. Ironic, eh?

Success involves the ability to plan ahead and delay gratification. Parents who want to prepare their children for success, therefore, should avoid indulging their whims.

Trying to protect children from frustration turns reality upside-down and inside-out. A child raised in this topsy-turvy manner will not, when the time comes, have the skills needed to deal with the often frustrating realities of life.

Children don't know what is in their own best interest. If they did, they wouldn't need parents for eighteen or more years, now would they?

The more parents try to make their children happy, the more they prevent their children from learning how to make, and keep, themselves happy.

You cannot tell, from your child's reaction, whether you have made a good decision or a bad one. A child will respond enthusiastically to very bad decisions and with great distress to very good ones.

Guilt is one reason parents give in to tantrums. To parents who mistakenly believe that the measure of good parenting is a constantly happy child, a tantrum says, "You're not doing a good job."

Parents should always pretend that they know what they're doing. So should the leader of a country. When the leader fails at this, we, the people, begin to feel insecure. So it is with children when parents are indecisive.

A child who can't take "no" for an answer always has parents who can't say it and mean it.

You cannot **demand** a child's attention; you can only **command** it. Parents who constantly demand are only demonstrating their inability to command.

Don't worry about treating children fairly. Remember that to a child, "fair" means "me first" with the biggest and best of everything.

Parents are to teach and set good example. Neither is possible unless children pay a great deal of attention to parents. Parents, therefore, should be the center of attention in their children's lives, not the other way around.

The child whose parents avoid confronting the discomfort of separation never receives complete, implicit permission to separate from them.

A child's expressions of frustration are in direct proportion to the quality of the parental decision. Therefore, when you make a decision that causes your child to express great frustration, you can be reasonably certain you made a good one.

The fewer toys and, therefore, the more space a child has in which to explore and create, the more successful the child will be at occupying his or her time.

The ultimate goal of raising children
is to help them out of our lives and into
successful lives of their own.

Play exercises all of the skills a child needs in order to become a fully competent individual. Play is a child's way of celebrating growing up.

If parents truly expect children to obey, children will obey. Some parents, however, instead of expecting their children to obey, only **wish** they would. This fantasy never comes true. Children are not here to grant their parents' wishes.

Don't ever say a child is "just" playing. That's like saying a surgeon is "just" operating or a pilot is "just" flying an airplane. Play is the essence of being a child.

You cannot be both a friend and an active parent at the same time. If you try to be a friend to your child, you will not be an effective parent. And years later, when it's possible to be a good friend, you won't know how.

The recent trend has been toward structuring the young child's time with organized sports, music lessons, and so on. This reflects the mistaken belief that these things are more "meaningful" than play, when exactly the opposite is true.

A child's bedtime is not for the child's sake, but for his or her parents' sake. Parents who understand this put children to bed not because those children supposedly "need their sleep," but because they, the parents, need **for them** to sleep.

Adults need to let kids have their games back. A grown man shouldn't dress in a coach's uniform unless he's being paid to do so.

Parents who always put their children first may be surprised to eventually discover that their children put them last.

From the time he or she is six weeks old, read to your child at least thirty minutes each day. Hold your child close. Have a wonderful time.

Good parenting emanates from the heart
and from the gut. From the heart springs
love; from the gut springs common-sense.

Give your children regular doses of
Vitamin "N," as in "No."

Good parenting doesn't come from the head. It's not a matter, in other words, of how much or how hard one **thinks**. If that was the case, the smartest people would be the best parents, and I've yet to see evidence of that.

As children grow older, parents must give them greater freedom, including greater freedom to make mistakes.

Most of a child's misbehavior has no explanation other than "he/she is a child." Nonetheless, some adults seem to think the more complex the explanation, the more valid it must be.

A child needs parents who act as if they are powerful enough to protect and provide for him under any and all circumstances. Confidence in parents "anchors" the child's life. Without that anchor, a child feels adrift.

Some parents dwell so much on the theoretical "causes" of their children's misbehavior that they end up doing absolutely nothing about it.

More than anything else, children need parents who know where they stand as well as where they want their children to stand.

Because it involves dwelling on the past, guilt inhibits creative action in the present. One of the most counter-productive things, therefore, you can do to either yourself or your child is feel guilty.

Respect in the parent-child relationship is a two-way street. Children show respect for parents by obeying them, and parents show respect for children by expecting them to obey.

An adult does not demonstrate power to a child by yelling or threatening. True power is calm and purposeful. In yelling or threatening, therefore, an adult admits weakness.

The most effective means of helping a child toward becoming a productive, responsible member of society is to assign him or her a regular, daily routine of chores around the home. Parents who fail to do so are neglecting their civic responsibilities.

DAILY GUIDE TO PARENTING   APR.3

Success involves the ability to tolerate frustration and failure. Therefore, parents should take care not to protect their children from either too much frustration or too much failure.

If you want your child to become a winner, then I have three old-fashioned suggestions: First, say "No" more often than you say "Yes"; second, assign him to a daily routine of chores; third, do not pay him, in any way, for doing them.

"Children should be seen and not heard" simply means that when a child enters a room occupied by adults who are in conversation, the child is to pay attention, not clamor for it. An excellent idea, I'd say.

Not long ago, parents understood that in rearing a child, they had obligations to both the child **and** the community. Unlike many a contemporary parent, they didn't pay so much attention to the tree that they lost sight of the forest.

A child should always be free to disagree, but never free to disobey. Parents who do not tolerate disagreement are sowing the seeds of adolescent rebellion.

When a child goes to school, he takes his parents with him in the form of their discipline, their expectations, and their values. Regardless of how often you visit your child's school, you're there every day.

"Because I said so" should never stifle discussion. It should be understood to mean that when all is said and done, the adult will make the decision, and right or wrong, everyone will have to live with it.

Within a family, the proper place for children is the backseat. Parents need to sit in the front seat, so they can keep their eyes on the road ahead.

It is impossible to uplift a child's point-of-view to that of an adult's. When an adult argues with a child, therefore, the adult must sink to the child's level, making it impossible for the child to look up to the adult.

It is not respectful to treat someone as either **more** or **less** than he or she truly is. Therefore, parents should treat their children as neither equals nor fools.

The Save-Your-Breath Principle:
Until a child is old enough to understand the "why?" of a parental decision, no amount of words will do. When the child is old enough, he'll be able to figure it out on his own. In either case, save your breath.

Relieved of the need to test authority, the obedient child is free to be curious, to explore, to invent — in short, to be as creatively independent as possible. For this reason, expecting obedience of a child is a demonstration of true respect.

Since 1950, thousands upon thousands of books on every conceivable aspect of childrearing have been published. Are we raising better children as a result? I think not.

Children who fear their parents don't
obey; they submit.

Children learn whatever you teach them, whether you've intended for them to learn it or not.

Obedient children are not fearful. They are self-confident, relaxed, and secure. Secure enough, even, to indulge in a certain amount of rebellion.

Concerning the misbehavior of children, both bribes and threats are self-fulfilling. The more parents do either, the more children will misbehave.

Obedience paves the road to maturity. Someone who fails, as a child, to learn to be obedient will forever travel a rough road.

Don't try and get your children to **cooperate** with you. Cooperation, after all, implies a state of equality. Instead, expect obedience.

DAILY GUIDE TO PARENTING   SEPT.20

Way back when children were children and parents were in charge, **strict** referred to adults who defined rules clearly and enforced them consistently — adults, in other words, who understood their obligations to children.

"Wait until your father gets home" can, on one hand, be an admission of weakness by a mother. Or, it can be an affirmation of solidarity between spouses concerning disciplinary matters. The difference depends on the follow-through.

Truly strict parents teach their children to expect no more out of a situation than they're willing to put into it. In other words, strict parents represent reality correctly to their children.

Children want to do their best. To motivate a child to do his or her best, never do for the child what the child is capable of doing on his or her own.

In ancient times, the "rod" was a symbol of royal authority. Therefore, "spare the rod, spoil the child" simply means that parents who, whether they spank or not, fail to exercise effective authority spoil — as in **ruin** — their children.

More often than not, the child whose parents say is "bored" in school is nothing more than lazy. He's had too much done for him, too much given to him, and too little expected of him.

By organizing a reality the child is not yet capable of organizing for himself, rules insure a child's physical and emotional well-being. In the absence of rules that are enforced "strictly," a child is at risk.

Thanks to "Sesame Street" and other supposedly educational children's programs, today's kids have the attitude that school should be a party, with Big Bird as master of ceremonies.

"To spank or not to spank" is not the question. The question, regardless of what discipline you choose, is simply this: "Does it accomplish what you want it to accomplish?"

The commandment that adults must make children "feel good about themselves" means adults can no longer tell children the whole truth about themselves or the things they do. The best truth, after all, often carries with it a bit of a sting.

Some folks say children who are spanked hate themselves for being rotten kids, learn that hitting others is okay, and will someday abuse their own children. That's true of children who are **beaten**, but not of children who are simply spanked.

DAILY GUIDE TO PARENTING   APR. 18

Parents who are there to catch their children every time they fall only set them up for bigger, more catastrophic tumbles.

It's possible to spank a child properly and have it accomplish something. The problem with spanking is that lots of parents make a sorry mess of it.

Teachers would rather have a class full of average-IQ kids, all of whom are **respectful, responsible,** and **resourceful,** than a class full of kids with IQ's over 150, but who are lacking in those "Three R's." If you don't believe me, ask a teacher.

When your child tells you that **all** his friends can do something you won't let him do, you need only say, "Well, then you're going to be the most special child in the neighborhood."

The biggest problem potential to a family in which there is, and will forever be, only one child is that the child may think the marriage is a three-some. In a marriage, three's a crowd.

There should never be any question about who's running the family circus. It is a child's inalienable right to be informed early in life that parents are the ringmasters.

Rosemond's Rule For Getting Along With Grandparents: When in Rome, do as the Romans do; when the Romans come to you, do as the Romans do.

Bobo, a little-known Chinese philosopher, once said: "When parent at a loss, child make bad boss."

When I was in school, you were penalized if your parents helped you with your science project. Today, you're penalized if they don't. Reality has turned upside-down for children, and the values it once held are pouring out like grains of sand.

The so-called "terrible" twos are all about the child's refusal to accept that after nearly two years of being the center of his parents' attention, he must now make them the center of his.

The idea that nearly all children of previous generations feared their parents is a myth. Believing this myth, this generation of parents has made darned sure their children don't fear them — or respect them, either.

The second eighteen months of life is the most precedent-setting of times in the parent-child relationship. What parents accomplish therein will never have to be accomplished again. What they don't accomplish will come back to haunt them.

For a generation or more, we adults have been giving children the impression that the only difference between us and them is one of height. And then we wonder why they call us by our first names.

Don't ever ask a child a question if you don't really mean for the child to have a choice in the matter.

The more "involved" a parent is with a child, the more the line between adult and child becomes blurred, making it almost impossible, when a crisis occurs, for the parent to see the child objectively and respond effectively.

Children need to be told what to do by parents who aren't afraid or embarrassed by an occasional showdown. Children feel most secure and comfortable with parents who know where they stand, and stand and deliver.

The more "involved" a parent is with a child, the more the line between adult and child becomes blurred, making it increasingly difficult for the child to look up to the parent.

The child who is disciplined as well as he or she is loved is a happy, healthy child.

Once upon a time, at-home women called themselves not "stay-at-home moms," but "housewives," thus referring to themselves as women whose primary relationships were with other adults, not children.

A balance of love and discipline create security for a child. Security forms the pad from which a child launches his or her life. The more solid the pad, the better able the child is to reach for the stars.

Parents should generally stay out of sibling squabbles. If they must get involved, they should do so such that both children are held equally responsible. No villain, no victim; therefore, no payoff; therefore, less reason to squabble.

Misbehavior attracts attention, putting a child center-stage in the family. The center of attention is addicting. To feed the "habit," the child must misbehave. This is the "snowball" of misbehavior, and once it gets going, it's very hard to stop.

How do you get a child to do what he's told the first time he's told? Don't ever repeat yourself.

The secure child has no compulsion to misbehave, no neurotic need to attract attention for the mere sake of attention. He is secure not only because his parents love him, but also because they discipline him well.

A child who is expected to perform daily tasks around the home — tasks which must be done properly or done over — will come to school prepared to accept and do his best with assignments from teachers.

When you have a disagreement with your spouse, you don't refer to it as "marital rivalry" do you? That's because there's no third party trying to make you get along, and if there was, you never would.

If your child is respectful, responsible, and resourceful, then regardless of which teacher he "draws", he'll make the very best of the situation.

The problem isn't that siblings have conflict, but that parents usually blame one child for "starting" it. As a result, the conflict between the siblings escalates as each tries, ever more desperately, to get the parents to blame the other.

The solution to most behavior problems lies not in understanding why a particular problem is occurring, but in doing something about it. I'm referring to nothing more than good, old-fashioned discipline.

There are two ways to avoid sibling conflict: First, don't have more than one child; second, if you have more than one, space them at least eighteen years apart.

Today's parents (and even many teachers) don't want learning to be frustrating for children. They don't realize that something earned through hard work can never be taken away, whereas that which comes easy is here today, gone tomorrow.

DAILY GUIDE TO PARENTING   AUG. 30

Children cause sibling conflict, parents cause sibling rivalry. One is inevitable, the other is not.

Yes, I'm an "expert" at rearing children. Their names are Eric and Amy, now young adults. You, too, can be an expert at rearing children — your own, no one else's.

Children need rules, routines, and daily responsibilities. These "Three R's" simplify their lives, promote security, and provide a stable framework within which creative freedom is possible.

We've been led to believe that people who go to graduate school know more about raising children than do grandmothers. In other words, a childrearing expert isn't someone who's reared children, but someone who thinks about it a lot. How absurd.

Consistency may be the oil, but variety is the spice of living. Don't limit your options by subscribing too literally to the idea that you must be consistent. The rules should be steady; the consequences of violating them can vary.

The term "working **mother**" implies that the woman in question is neglecting her children. When she gets home, therefore, she has to make up for her absence by paying them lots of attention. This is myth, not fact, and a very destructive myth at that.

A child without rules is like a fish
out of water.

While watching television, a child is not exercising any important skill. The child's creative abilities are, in effect, shut down. Television-watching, therefore, is a deprivational experience for children.

My mother didn't give me a lot of attention, yet I never doubted her love. By not becoming highly involved with me, she gave me complete permission to emancipate myself from her. She truly loved me; therefore, she was willing to let me go.

Where toilet training is concerned, it's as unwise to try and "push the river" as it is to "jump the gun." Come to think of it, this same advice applies to a lot of things parents need to help children accomplish.

If parents teach, but children don't learn,
the problem is with the teaching method,
not the student.

In trying to be both a friend and a parent, you will fail at both. The better a parent you are for eighteen years or so, the better friends you and your child will be from that point on. Put first things first.

The idea that a lot of physical closeness between parent and child can keep a child immature is groundless. The opposite is true: the more secure a child feels in his parents' love, the more readily he will move away from them when the time comes.

When He made babysitters, God intended for them to be employed on a regular basis. The full commandment is "be fruitful, multiply, get a sitter, go out for the evening."

A Poem: After crawling, don't confine,
Child-proof for your peace of mind.
Allow your child to freely roam,
In the safety of your home.

Children are fascinated by adult relationships and the things adults do. They are not, on the other hand, fascinated by adults who pay a lot of attention to **them**. You want your child to pay attention to you? Have relationships! Have a life!

Parents tend to exaggerate the significance of a toddler's inevitable tantrums. Suffice it to say that when adults make mountains out of a child's molehills, the child will learn to build molehills into mountains.

In the adult-centered family, the major share of attention goes from adult to adult rather than adult to child. This "weans" children from the need for constant attention, thus permitting the growth of self-reliance.

The importance of putting a child to bed is so daddies and mommies can be husbands and wives again. Bedtime is an exercise in separating the child from the marriage.

It's not necessary that you always answer a young child's questions "correctly," only that you answer them in ways the child can understand. If "correct" was necessary, we'd read to children from the encyclopedia instead of from story books.

Grandma's Rule: When the child has done what he's **supposed** to do, the child may do what he **wants** to do.

Self-confident parents accept their own imperfections as no big deal. Their children, therefore, come to see them not as ideal, but real; faulted, but blameless. As such, their children are better able to come to grips with the realities of life.

Forty years ago, a woman with children who worked outside of her home was referred to as a working **wife**. Today, she is called a working **mother** — one example of how today's woman is encouraged to put her children before her relationship with her husband.

The only parent who cannot admit
to having made a mistake to his or her
child, who cannot make apology to
the child, is a parent lacking in
self-confidence.

A child watching television is not learning to be a winner. He's learning how to be a spectator instead of a doer, a follower rather than a leader.

Consistency doesn't mean always delivering the same consequence for any given misbehavior. It means that regardless of the consequence they choose, parents never fail to communicate their no-uncertain-terms disapproval of that misbehavior.

Most of a young child's "lies" are told because adults ask questions to which they already know the answers.

The ability to develop self-control depends upon being able to accurately predict the consequences of your own behavior. That's why parental consistency is so important. Without it, a child wanders lost.

Respect for self, without which true happiness is unattainable, begins with respect for others.

In order to develop self-respect, a child must first develop respect for his or her parents. This gradually extends to other adults and eventually to all of creation. Only then is genuine self-respect possible. What goes around, comes around.

Respect for others, without which true success is unattainable, begins with respect for one's parents.

In how they raise children, parents have obligations to both their children **and** the community. Among other effects, the **nouveau** idea that parents should give children lots of attention has made parents less attentive to their community obligations.

DAILY GUIDE TO PARENTING   AUG. 14

If you make a decision which causes your child to yell "It's not fair!", you must have done something right. Keep on doing it.

A culture is defined and stabilized by it's childrearing traditions. Tinkering with a culture's childrearing traditions, as we have done over the last forty years, destabilizes both the family and the culture. For proof of this, look around you.

From a child's point of view, parents exist for one of two reasons: either to pay attention **to** him, or be paid attention to **by** him. Which conclusion the child arrives at is completely up to his parents.

How to get revenge for years of sibling conflict: When it comes time to pay for college educations, each spouse should point at the other and whine, "Make him/her do it!"

The term the **child-centered family**, which came into vogue in the 1970's, is the most anti-child, anti-family, anti-culture concept "helping" professionals have ever spun from the whole cloth of their childrearing rhetoric.

Two unrelated children will work cooperatively on just about any task assigned them; but two siblings will argue and accuse and complain about one another endlessly. So, for the sake of your sanity, never assign siblings to the same job.

Aren't we parents foolish?
We often expect a child to know the difference between right and wrong long before he knows the difference between right and left.

All meaningful learning comes about by trial and error. A youngster learns to take responsible control of his/her life by making mistakes. A parent's job is not to always prevent them, but to make sure the child learns from them.

In the last forty years, parents have grown increasingly dependent upon the professional "expert" for childrearing advice. As a result, they're in grave danger of losing complete touch with their own common-sense.

The more restrictions parents try to put on a teenager's choice of friends, the more deceptive the teen will become. A restrictive approach almost always creates more problems than it solves.

Parents who are constantly obsessed with making intellectually "correct" childrearing decisions wind up failing to do anything decisive at all.

When a child misbehaves, keep your reprimand to twenty-five words or less. A few words have a much better chance of sinking in than a lot.

As a parent, you will not always make the very best decisions. Nonetheless, you will almost always make better decisions than your child would make for himself. In the final analysis, the rare exceptions become irrelevant.

Over the last forty years, the "experts" have done a darned good job of replacing childrearing realities with "parenting" rhetoric.

Parents who constantly bend over backwards for their children eventually fall over backwards.

To paraphrase The Book of Ecclesiastes, there's a time for giving a child attention, and a time for getting it from the child. If you give too much, you'll get too little in return.

Parents who always go out of their way for their children eventually lose their way.

It is impossible for a child to successfully emancipate himself from the center of attention in the family. Who wants to give up the spotlight?

Parents who are willing to pay the penalty — emotionally or otherwise — for their children's irresponsible behavior should have no problem figuring out why their children continue to behave irresponsibly.

One of the most significant signs of healthy emotional development in a three-year-old is the ability to be self-occupied — without making unnecessary requests for adult attention — for relatively long periods of time.

Many of today's children are addicted to toys. Not just the toys themselves, mind you, but to the **getting** of toys. The ritual trip to the toy store has become an end in itself.

Just as there is no perfect child, just as there is no perfect parent, there is no perfect means of discipline. Do your best.

There has never been, and will never be a democratic family. Parents have two options: either establish a benevolent dictatorship or throw wide the door to anarchy.

"Strong-willed child" implies that disobedience is a matter of some inbred temperamental trait. While it is true that some children are more difficult than others, persistent disobedience is a parenting problem, not a child problem.

To paraphrase President Kennedy, parents should raise children who eventually realize that what's of ultimate importance is not what their families do for them, but what they do for their families.

It is said that horses and dogs know when a human is even the least bit insecure around them. When they sense insecurity, they refuse to obey. How much more perceptive and intelligent is a human child than a horse or a dog?

Children are far more likely to give their parents problems than they are their teachers. This is Number 39 of the Fifty Ways to Grieve Your Mother: Be the teacher's perfect precious and bite Mommy on the leg — or better yet, her ego.

If you put your children first, they will surely put themselves first as well.

When parents make a child's life into a bowl of cherries, the child will almost certainly, as an adult, be forever in the pits.

The young child must be convinced of his parents' ability to provide for and protect him under any and all circumstances. To the degree that he trusts in their ability to do so, he will feel secure and will be able to discover self-esteem.

If you want your child to take care of what you give him, hand him nothing on a silver platter.

Being married is the hardest thing there is. Comparatively, raising children is a piece of cake. Folks who think raising children is hard are probably paying too much attention to their children and not enough to their marriages.

Family meals are an opportunity to reaffirm the values of sharing and unity. It matters little what people eat or how much; good conversation and the feeling that "we are one for all, and all for one" are what count.

Many parents mistakenly believe that consistency is a matter of willpower. Not so. It's a matter of planning. One cannot discipline consistently until one has a plan, something with which to be consistent.

Children suck their thumbs simply because it feels good. Thumbsucking is a portable source of pleasure, always right on hand! The answer to why some children suck their thumbs and others don't is simply "because."

If you disagree with an "expert" on some aspect of childrearing, give yourself the benefit of the doubt.

By getting upset at the small things children do, parents set the stage for repeat performances. Once the stage is set, children play the parts assigned them.

I've never understood why parents are told to "never spank in anger." I can't imagine anything more confusing to a child than to be spanked by someone who is displaying no emotion.

In order to establish that they are in charge, parents must slowly but surely dismantle a toddler's fantasy — arrived at honestly — that he or she is the center of the universe. Screams and protests are inevitable.

Parents who try hard to please their children are in danger of raising children who are not pleasing.

Authoritarian parents refuse to accept that children have minds of their own. **Authoritative** parents, on the other hand, not only accept the fact, but celebrate it!

Parents who try hard to please their children quickly lose sight of what's pleasing to themselves.

A common-sensical approach to childrearing is not, by any means, unthinking. It is simply un-intellectual. Common sense comes from the heart and the gut, not from the head.

When a husband becomes a father,
and a wife becomes a mother, it becomes
a simple matter for a child to step
between that which is already divided,
and conquer.

Discipline is not the sum of a set of methods. It is a climate of understanding that permeates every aspect of the family's life.

The real danger to children in watching television is not so much **what** they watch, but the accumulated effect of the very process of **watching**. Keep in mind that **all** television programs — regardless of content — are watched in the same do-nothing way.

Letting a child be the center of attention in a family prolongs self-centeredness indefinitely, and nothing is quite as unattractive in an adult (or a child, for that matter) as self-centeredness.

When a child is paid for doing chores, those chores are not a means of contributing to the family; rather, they become a means of **blackmailing** the family.

With the exception of breast-feeding, there is nothing mothers do that fathers cannot do just as well.

When parents pay a child for performing chores, they create the illusion that if ever the child doesn't want the money, he doesn't have to do the chores.

Letting children be the center of attention in a family teaches them that self-worth is a function of how much attention they receive from other people.

To prove to yourself that chores bond a child to a family's values, ask, "Where in America have family values been handed down most reliably from generation to generation?" The answer: In farming areas, where from early on, children do chores.

Letting children be the center of attention in a family turns the family upside down, inside out, and backwards.

Democracy between parent and child is impossible. You can create the **illusion** of democracy through clever use of words, but getting to the bottom of things, you'll find that one or the other has the final word. God help them both if it's the child.

Parents who refuse to child-proof, who view a toddler's determination to "get into everything" as a test of their authority, only wind up frustrating themselves as well as the child.

The difference between "experts" and parents is that experts talk about things parents can't see, while parents see things experts never talk about.

Unless parents are consistent with their discipline, a child cannot predict consequences, and a child who cannot predict consequences cannot become self-disciplined.

In the 1970s, we accepted into our vernacular the phrase "child-centered family" not realizing that when a child is the center of his parents' attention, their relationship is in jeopardy.

Consistency is more a matter of always demonstrating the same **attitude** toward a child's misbehavior than a matter of always using the same technique.

When children squabble, the easiest thing for them to do is run to an adult for help. Because it's easiest, it also involves the least amount of thought. When an adult cooperates with a tattle-tale, therefore, the adult is encouraging the child not to think.

DAILY GUIDE TO PARENTING   JULY 15

The themes that dominate the parent-child relationship when the child is two are the same themes that dominate the relationship during the child's early and middle teen years. The "twos" are just practice.

A child who frequently says "I'm bored!" actually means, "Mom and Dad, in buying me all these toys, you caused me to believe play came from a toy store. Otherwise, I'd have learned that play comes from (pointing now to his head) right up here."

A father's contribution to his children is primarily a measure of how much he adores their mother.

Parents who are willing to pay the penalty when their children behave irresponsibly should have no problem figuring out why those children continue to behave irresponsibly.

Good discipline doesn't have to be complicated. Rather, it must be well organized, easily communicated, and easily dispensed. The simpler, the better.

It is part of a child's responsibility to himself to rebel, and it is his parents' fundamental responsibility to contain that rebellion within safe limits.

Should parents give reasons to children? Of course! Should parents attempt to reason with children? Not if they want to keep their wits about them.

Yesterday's "undisciplined brat" is today's "hyperactive" or "strong-willed" child. Children haven't changed at all, but the rhetoric has.

How much freedom should a teenager have? More than parents are comfortable giving, but less than the teen wants.

The job of raising children is never too big for one person; if the one person's big enough for the job, that is.

The answers to such questions as "at what age is it okay for a teenager to start dating?" are determined by looking carefully at the teenager, not the calendar.

Parents influence the future through their worries, their anxieties, their fears, all of which tend to be self-fulfilling. In this respect, all parents are amateur fortune-tellers.

A spanking is a spanking only if (a) the spanking is done by hand, (b) the hand strikes the child's rear end only, and (c) the hand strikes no more than twice. Anything else is a beating.

If you want to spank less and more effectively, then you must spank as a **first resort**. The more spontaneous a spanking is, and the more quickly it is over and done with, the longer it will last.

Sleeping in his or her own bed affirms that a child is an independent, autonomous individual. As such, it helps a child develop a clearly separate identity and therefore a clearer sense of self-esteem.

Every threat is empty. And children, being the intuitively brilliant little people that they are, know it.

Aggressive toddlers don't have bad parents, nor is anything wrong with them. At this age, most aggressive behavior — no matter how "uncivilized" — is perfectly normal. Well, not **perfectly** normal, but normal just the same.

Every child needs to experience the value of contributing to the family in the form of chores, and every child needs to learn the value of a dollar. Parents need to make sure, therefore, that the twain rarely, if ever, meet.

Sharing is one of those civilized things, like chewing with one's mouth closed, that parents are in a hurry for children to acquire. Unfortunately, children are in no equal hurry.

Children who are paid for doing everyday chores around the home learn neither the value of money nor the value of contribution. Their citizenship is therefore impaired.

The worst of times, the best of times. That description fits no other stage of human growth and development as well as it does the "twos." Except maybe the "teens." Come to think of it, they're pretty much the same.

The Declaration of Independence says we have a right to **pursue** happiness, not a right to happiness itself. This means parents cannot give children good self-esteem; rather, they can only help their children discover it for themselves.

A child will not pay sufficient attention to a parent who is acting as if it is his or her foremost obligation to pay attention to the child.

A child learns who he is by first having it defined for him who his parents are, and who, therefore, he is not. Stated another way, a child discovers his own place by first being told where it cannot be.

The marriage preceeds the children and was meant to succeed them.

The Three C's of Good Communication:

(1) Be **commanding** as opposed to demanding.

(2) Be **concise** as opposed to long-winded.

(3) Be **concrete** as opposed to obscure.

Good communication will prevent many a discipline problem.

DAILY GUIDE TO PARENTING   JULY2